G000081919

BEDMINSTER
· BETWEEN THE WARS ·

BEDMINSTER
· BETWEEN THE WARS ·

Profile of a local community 1918-1939

Leonard Vear

Published for Bristol & West Building Society
by Redcliffe Press, Bristol

First published in 1981 by
REDCLIFFE PRESS LTD
14 Dowry Square, Bristol 8

Printed in Great Britain by

The Bristol & West Building Society

ISBN 0 905459 38 5

Contents

Introduction

From the historical point of view, Bedminster has a greater allegiance to Somerset than to Bristol, as the old Hundred of Hareclive and Bedminster comprised a large part of North Somerset, south of the Avon. The parishes of Barrow, Butcombe, Backwell, Chelvey and Nemnet and Winford, were all within its boundaries. Over the years, political and administrative expediency have reduced old Bedminster to the status of a Bristol suburb. In fact, during the 1970s, it was suggested (to the horror of Bedminster people) that the name of 'Bedminster' be replaced by 'Bristol South'. Fortunately, this did not materialise. Even so, old Bedminster, to the outsider, is hidden under the names of Southville, Ashton Gate, Ashton, Headley Park and Hartcliffe. However, local historians and the older inhabitants of Bedminster still regard these districts, together with Totterdown, Knowle and Bishopsworth, as Bedminster. And so, in these pages, they are considered as such.

This book would not have been possible without the kind help and co-operation of numerous Bedminster people. I would like to thank the following for giving me their time and memories of Bedminster between the wars.

The Adams sisters; Miss D. Alcock; Eddie Best; Len Carey; Mr and Mrs Cogan (née Stephens); the late Albert Hilton and Ada Hilton; Ernie Janes (S.B.C.C.); Charlie Symes; Mary Munden; Len Portch; Mr and Mrs Fred Wedlock; Ernie Wheeler; Sydney Wookey; Roy Smith; Don West; John Miles and Edwin Vear.

Also, Don Loader, Les Tovey and Reece Winstone for their help with photographs and last, but not least, Ted Houghton, whose liaison work on my behalf was invaluable.

Thanks also to friends and fellow members of the Malago Society and members of the Salvation Army.

1 The Mean Streets

The Great War was over; peace had been celebrated on Bristol's streets. With a beaming face of benevolence, the Board of Guardians of Long Ashton Workhouse decided that one of the workhouse pigs be killed to provide a roast dinner for the inmates, in addition to their having sugar in their tea and an allowance of tobacco. The children had cake at tea-time.

But for some it was a time of sadness, in the knowledge that husbands, sons and lovers would never return. Women were to mourn and regret the absence of their men-folk in the hard times that lay ahead.

During the transitional period from war to peace there was little noticeable change in the appearance of old Bedminster from that of the turn of the century. Through East Street, traffic made its leisurely way towards Ashton and Bedminster Down: handcarts, single horse or pony-drawn carts and delivery wagons with their large 'Shires'. Bicycles far out-numbered the scattering of cars and motor-bikes. Trams bounced and clattered their way along sunken, metal tracks, spring-loaded arms reaching upwards from the open top-deck, to connect with overhead power lines. Pedestrians walked and talked their way along the thoroughfare, often upon the road itself, for the noisy trams could be heard in good time, the slower horse-drawn vehicles easily avoided. The aftermath of war showed in the shortage of young men, the war-disabled and, in the local press, lists of ex-servicemen asking for work.

Bedminster boasted some 18 public houses between Bedminster Bridge (shown here in 1933) and the London Inn.

The Ashton tram outside Wills' Factory in East Street, Bedminster, taking about 100 yards to come to a halt after reaching 18 m.p.h. or so between stops.

Behind the commercial façade of shops – and Bedminster's boast of some 18 public houses between Bedminster Bridge and the *London Inn* – lay the Victorian legacy of tightly terraced houses with little or no garden. There were squalid courts where families shared not only a single water-tap, but also a common outside-toilet. One tenement in St. John's Buildings (a narrow lane which had its exit through an archway to Bedminster Parade) consisted of two rooms only. The living-room downstairs, a single bedroom above. The latter could only be reached by outside stairs.

Housing conditions in such areas were recognised by the Public Health Department in its annual reports and did not go without comment. A definition of a 'fit' house was that it had to be free from serious dampness; be adequately lighted and ventilated; be properly drained and provided with necessary sanitary conveniences and a suitable arrangement for disposing of slop water; be in good repair; have a satisfactory water supply; an adequate accommodation for washing purposes and a well ventilated store for food.

A large number of houses adjacent to the tanneries and the glue factory in Stillhouse Lane lacked many of the required amenities. Because of the abnormal housing shortage in the early twenties, repair work was carried out on buildings which normally would have been pulled down. Some owners did not charge their tenants an economical rent in the erroneous belief that not to do so exempted them from carrying out necessary repairs to their property. On the other hand, some tenants tolerated this position as long as their rents were not raised. However, where owners were taking advantage of the accommodation shortage to raise rents to two, or three times, the pre-war level (although this did not always show on the rent book) tenants were sub-letting parts of the houses at double the amount of rent they themselves had to pay.

In the report a plea was made for houses to be built in conjunction with local authorities, together with the suggestion that perhaps employers of labour should realise that industrial unrest among their employees might be due, in part, to unsatisfactory housing conditions.

A street of tightly terraced Victorian houses in festive mood for the Silver Jubilee of 1935 — Willway Street.

A former inhabitant of Willway Street recalls those days:

'Chickens and ducks were kept in the small backyard – chiefly for our own use. There was an outside toilet, flushed by throwing a bucket of water down after use. Sometimes this went over the wooden seat which wasn't very comfortable for the next person.

'We used candles and paraffin lamps for lighting; later gas.

'In Waters Place (known locally as Murder Alley) they shared toilets and tap-water.

'Our kitchen was separate from the house. It was the lower part of a small extension. Above it was a small bedroom to which access was gained only through a larger bedroom. The kitchen being as it was, food had to be carried across the open yard into the house. We found it convenient to leave the downstairs window open, at mealtimes, so we could pass the food through. It kept warmer that way.'

In the poorer type of dwelling one of the greatest inconveniences for the housewife was the lack of space for washing and drying clothes. In some houses the usual method of heating water was in a stone or copper basin, set in brick, underneath which a fire was lit. Then came the back-breaking task of putting the dripping clothes through the mangle's wooden rollers, laboriously rotated by a large, cast-iron handwheel.

For many years there had been private wash-houses in the district, open to the public for a fee, but after the opening of the Mayors Paddock Baths in 1873, better facilities were made available at that place for washing and ironing clothes. Hot and cold water was supplied and each customer had a place to herself in which to dry the washing. Some women took the opportunity to wash for others, thus earning themselves a few shillings.

In the houses on Windmill Hill, for example, where the rooms were more spacious, clothes were usually dried in front of the fire during the inclement months of winter. A room-wide, wooden-railed clothes airer hung suspended from the ceiling and over this the clothes were draped. Heavy, solid flat-irons were placed on the fire to heat and had their bottoms wiped with a cloth before being applied to the linen.

And while the necessity for public financed housing was being bruited, at the same time warning was given that to suddenly propel slum-dwellers into modern, commodious accommodation, with a large garden, was not without its dangers.

The truth of this became apparent, in the late twenties, when people were moved from such areas as Waters' Place, Hope Square and Sargent Street, to the new council estate at Knowle West. The more intimate way of life of old Bedminster was missed. There was a feeling of isolation, generated to some extent by the lack of resources, such as money (for many were unemployed) and no preparation as to how to cope with, or adapt to, a new way of life. A lack of amusement centres – cinemas, theatres and clubs – gave rise to hooliganism and crime which gave that district a bad name for many years to follow.

2 A home of one's own

In the preceding pages the worst side of Bedminster's housing was dealt with. However, existing at the same time as these slum properties were the more attractive late Victorian terraced homes, as in the Windmill Hill, Southville, St John's Lane, Totterdown, Lower Knowle, Ashton Gate, the Chessels and Bedminster Down areas. These bay-windowed houses exist to this day. Interspersed amongst their ranks were the grander houses of professional and business people, such as those behind St Paul's Church, in Acraman's Road and Alpha Road and Cranby House in St John's Road. Later development saw the larger houses of Knowle and Bishopsworth surrounded by new estates.

The building of new houses, both council and private, accelerated and the general trend for saving and house purchase through building societies showed that, nationally, members of building societies numbering some 625,013 in 1918, had increased to 1,416,456 by 1927. While there might seem to be a paradox here, with people buying their own homes at a time when there was an economic depression, many of those buying were in what was considered to be stable employment; in the tobacco industry, Robinson's and the railways, for example. Considering such an investment was wise, when housing was comparatively cheap.

In 1929 older property was for sale at the following typical prices:

Southville. A three-bedroomed, double-bay villa. £85 down and balance of £375 accepted at £3/10s per month.

Totterdown. £435 asked. £100 down accepted.

This Bristol & West Building Society advertisement appeared in the early thirties.

In 1932 modern houses were being offered in St John's Lane for £25 deposit, while an older type of house in Monmouth Street, Victoria Park, was available for £295.

By the end of the 1930s several new estates had been built in the area, Lower Knowle and Knowle being greatly extended, with southern development at Ashton Gate. At Headley Park, where development took place in the mid-1930s, a house was available for £360, with a deposit of £25 and repayments at 9/2d (46p) per week. In addition, the Redcliffe Furnishing Company offered £5 worth of furniture free to those who purchased a house!

That there was confidence that the trend for house purchase would continue during the 1930s, is evidenced by the fact that the Bristol & West Building Society opened its first branch office at Cannon Street, Bedminster, in 1931.

The original premises were in the building next door to the present one. The second branch manager, Mr. E. S. Streets who is now 85 years old, ran both this and the Gloucester Road, Bishopston, branch in the 1930s. He remembers that business was brisk in Bedminster and he used to put the day's 'takings' in the Wills' factory safe in East Street.

Bristol & West's present Transport Manager, Mr. Bill Pollard, worked as relief manager at Cannon Street just before the Second World War. He recalls working longer hours in those days, with the office staying open until 7.00 p.m. on Mondays, and only half-an-hour for lunch each day. Wednesday afternoons were always quiet with the shops being closed; the busiest time was the lunch hour when workers from Wills', Robinson's and Colodense used to queue up to make their mortgage payments or small investments – just a few pounds here and there.

More spacious and attractive housing in the Southville area, circa 1918.

This fine, early Georgian mansion stood in Parson Street at the foot of Nover's Hill. The Bristol-born Poet Laureate Robert Southey spent many happy hours here when it was his grandmother's home.

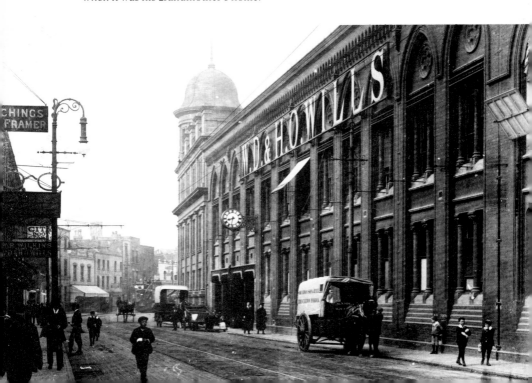

3 Earning a living

The aim of thousands of Bedminster children who left school in the twenties and thirties was to find employment with one of the major Bristol firms. Top of the list was W.D. & H.O. Wills, followed by Robinson's, Mardon's and Fry's.

Wills was the largest employer of local labour and to obtain work at one of their factories 'set you up for life, as long as you kept your nose clean.' The company's first Bedminster factory had opened in East Street in 1886, followed by another at Ashton Gate in 1900.

Girls making cigarettes by hand at Wills' in the 1920s. Each girl has a weighing balance on top of her desk.

Cleanliness and a neat appearance were among the criteria looked for in recruits. No doubt the management believed that a sloppy appearance foreshadowed sloppy work. Male employees were expected to wear a collar and tie at all times and to be reasonably well-shaven. Another minor facet of discipline was explained by a former employee at the East Street factory:

'Until I was married I had to call the foreman "Mister", but after I was married, at 23, I was allowed to call him Frank. The crazy thing was that another workmate, well over 50 and unmarried, still had to call the foreman "Mister".'

The main source of employment in Bedminster in the 1920s and 1930s was W.D. & H.O. Wills.

Girls who applied for work had to produce, in addition to a reference from their local church or chapel, a sample of needle-work. This, no doubt, was to prove their sense of concentration and application, essential to the rather monotonous routine of production. It was also the rule, between the wars, that upon marriage girls left their employment. An exception was made in the case of widows.

Apart from continuity of employment there were many other advantages in working for Wills: medical treatment at the factory site, a convalescent home and a sanatorium, plus the extensive facilities of an Athletic Club. In addition, an Evening Club at Luckwell Road provided opportunities for billiards, cards, skittles, bagatelle, chess, table-tennis and a miniature rifle range. There were also clubs for angling, swimming and amateur dramatics.

A year's full service entitled the employee to one week's holiday with full pay and there was a pension upon retirement. And, what was most appreciated, a yearly bonus which was not regarded as such but as a gift, based on the yearly profits. It takes little imagination to see why a job in Wills was held in such high esteem.

The Lord Mayor, Ald. Walter Bryant, welcomes the Mayor of Rouen to Wills' during British-French Week in June, 1930.

Until 1923 a minority found employment at the South Liberty Lane Pit, at the lower part of Bedminster Down. Three shifts were worked: 6 a.m. to 2 p.m.; 2 p.m. to 10 p.m. and 10 p.m. to 6 a.m. In a good week the miner could earn £3.00, but usually the wage was below this. The mining industry in Bedminster is still commemorated by two pubs, *The Miners' Arms* on Bedminster Down Road and *The Jolly Colliers* in West Street.

Other 'dirty' jobs were to be had at local tanneries and at Capper Pass Smelting Works. The tramways and railways, while offering regular employment, had the disadvantage of unsociable hours but this was offset, to some extent, by the free uniforms the companies supplied.

It was not unusual for sons to follow their fathers onto the railways. Youths began as cleaners in the engine sheds and sometimes had the job of cycling around to the homes of firemen and drivers to wake them up for an early shift. It was while coming home early one morning in 1926 that "Tinker" West, a railway worker living on Windmill Hill, discovered St Michael's and All Angels' Church on fire. He knocked up the vicar at the Frazer Street vicarage, but in spite of the efforts of the fire brigade, the church was gutted. The ground on which the church stands was given by Alfred Capper Pass and, after the fire, his son, Douglas, replaced the choir stalls formerly given to the church by his father.

There was a strong economic relationship between local industry and Bedminster's shops and this was especially so in the case of Wills. (More recently this has been seen with the removal of the East Street factory production to Hartcliffe, with a marked decline in local business.) It is, of course, only possible to give a selection of the old shops. These were usually family businesses, and there was a marked personal relationship between shopkeeper and customer. It was an essential part of the community, giving it a family quality more akin to a village. Thus was developed over the years a strong community with which the local inhabitants could and did identify themselves. So much so that adverse criticism was resented and outside intrusion, in the form of newcomers, was often begrudgingly accepted. The shop-keeper/customer alliance was often sorely tried when times were hard but some shopkeepers supplied their old customers with groceries, bread and meat on credit. Such was their trust that they would be paid when conditions made it possible.

Bosley's of Bedminster Down Road was the largest baker in the area (1920s).

Wintle's in West Street was a typical small family grocer. The two trace horses at the front of the cart were probably used to haul a heavy load up from Ashton (1920s).

The same cart, horse and driver as above at the White Horse in West Street. This time they are travelling, empty, towards Ashton (1920s).

A greengrocer's in St John's Lane in the 1930s. The stock is much the same as today but the prices are enormously different.

Shops which have lingered in the memories of many Bedminster people are Collard's the butcher, originally at Poet's Corner, North Street; Moden's the pork butcher, also in North Street and Babbage's the East Street butcher where cattle were driven through the shop to be slaughtered at the rear.

Bessant's had several confectionery shops in the area and Warbutton's Brandy Snap factory was just off East Street, at the rear of Robinson's factory.

The Bedminster Co-op proved extremely popular with the average family, mainly because of the 'divi' of one shilling and eightpence for every £1.00 spent in the shops. This form of easy saving took trade away from some businesses.

Bosley's of Bedminster Down Road had been there since 1897 and they were to be one of the largest bakeries in the area for many years.

For simple delicacies you went to Fluke's delicatessen in East Street or, not far away, was Bryant's small fronted shop, displaying cockles, mussels, crabs and other shellfish. For the less fastidious there were snails.

1927 saw the opening of Verrecchia's Ice-cream Parlour. Cones were a half-penny and a penny and a dish of ice-cream, with flavouring, two-pence, as also was a glass of coffee. Vans went out, in the thirties, to the surrounding streets and local people brought out their basins for a couple of pennies-worth.

'Some would bring out their largest basin so that a couple of pennies-worth would seem insignificant at the bottom of the basin. Naturally you were inclined to put in more than you should.'

Wintle's in West Street and Plaster's in St John's Lane were typical of small family grocers.

One of the largest draper's shops at that time was E. N. Miles, in Cannon Street. Actually there were three separate, but adjacent shops. Established in 1896, they were to finally close down in January 1981. They were drapers in the broadest sense selling anything from pins to carpets. Their good relationship with their customers ensured that many who left the immediate vicinity often came back to Miles' to do their shopping – from as far afield as North Somerset.

Customers' deliveries were effected by a delivery-boy on a bike, though in more recent years a van was used.

Alfred Beer's ladder store in North Street (1930s).

4 In sickness and in health

Under the 1911 Health Insurance Act manual workers and those not earning more than £160 per year, (later extended to £250 and then to £420), contributed towards unemployment and sickness benefits. This entitled the wage earner to free medicines, the services of a panel doctor, but not free hospital treatment. Nor was there any help for dependants, apart from a maternity grant of some thirty shillings. Those who were able paid for treatment, while many less well off patients were visited by the hospital almoner who, after assessing their personal circumstances, determined what he or she thought the patient was capable of paying.

In 1920 the insurance contribution was 10d a week for men and 9d for women, of which the employer paid 5d in each case.

A worker who fell ill and was off work had some financial entitlement but as this was insufficient to meet the needs of the whole family, more often than not he returned to work before fully fit. However, by joining one of the many friendly societies and paying a small weekly contribution, it was possible to make up some of the wages lost through illness. It was, for some, a way of saving money for a dividend was paid out at the end of the year to those who had not claimed benefits.

As there was no free dental treatment few working-class people visited a dentist until driven to do so. Thus, bad teeth led to undesirable eating habits which in turn led to bad health. One dentist, near Bristol Bridge, encouraged people to call, on Saturdays only, to have their teeth pulled free. Many Bedminster people took advantage of this – at least once – even though the treatment was a practice session for students. The operation was generally carried out without an anaesthetic for, in the 'thirties, this cost about two shillings and sixpence, cocaine one shilling and sixpence. Local children could have dental treatment at a Local Health Clinic in Dean Lane.

One of the real fears of the poor was the considered degradation of being 'buried on the Parish' (by the local Public Assistance Committee). It was a matter of pride that families bore the expense of burying their own. So, from the moment of birth, most people were insured for a penny or so a week to provide for their burial. Often several members of a family took out insurances on their parents, not only to cover the costs of burial but also to buy for themselves black dresses and dark suits for the occasion. Premiums were collected weekly at the door by insurance agents.

The Bristol Poor People's Dispensary had a branch in Malago Road, Bedminster, at the corner of Little Paradise. Like all dispensaries of this kind, it was set up to provide out-of-hospital treatment.

The work of the dispensaries was made possible by private subscription. For one guinea the subscriber received a book of five notes which could be given entire to those of his choice, as 'free' notes, or divided and used as a note of recommendation, the patient paying half-a-crown for treatment upon presenting it at the dispensary. The notes also covered midwifery and medical attendance on payment of five shillings.

By 1929 many business firms were buying notes for the benefit of their employees.

The first antenatal clinic was opened in West Street, Bedminster, on August 19th, 1920 and subsequently every Thursday. Here, working-class mothers were soon to appreciate the help given to them by the woman Medical Officer and Health Visitors. Minor treatment was given but more complicated cases were referred to either a private practitioner or one of the local hospitals. No charge of any kind was made.

The atmosphere was not so awesome as that of the hospital and therefore more acceptable to the mothers for the personal and intimate service provided. Those attending came to realise that to be healthy was not just having the ability to carry out household chores. Nagging conditions previously endured by many, such as anaemia, headaches, constipation, bad teeth, gynaelogical ailments and bad legs were shown to be curable and it was seen that treatment could bring about a vast improvement in general well-being. However, when a condition needed lengthy treatment, or a spell in hospital, many wives gave family needs priority and carried on, much as before, to the detriment of their own health.

Classes were held where systematic instruction was given in mother-craft, infant health, home management, cookery, sewing and knitting, together with maternity classes for expectant mothers.

The Bedminster Health Centre in St John's Lane was opened in 1937. It was a typical example of an up-to-date district clinic. Apart from family supervision, the clinic catered for school children attending twenty-four schools in the neighbourhood and provided the maternity services and child-welfare services for South Bristol and Knowle.

The Knowle Open-Air School, originally run by private subscription and taken over by the Council in 1920, had some 140 pupils. Children were recommended for admission by the doctor of School Medical and Tuberculosis Staff and by other doctors. There was a nurse permanently attached to the school.

In like vein were the Open Air Classes held in the bandstands of St George, Eastville and Bedminster parks all the year round, each accommodating 25 delicate children. The important factor in ensuring a high attendance at these classes was the close proximity of the schools to the children's homes.

With medical treatment expensive to the average person it was a familiar sight to see people with defective eyesight buying 'reading' glasses at Woolworths. The spectacles were heaped on the counter and the customer tried them on and tested their suitability with a displayed reading chart. They cost about sixpence.

Many resorted to old established home remedies. For boils there was a bread poultice or, rather more drastic in its effect, the neck of a heated bottle was placed over the swelling. When the air inside the bottle cooled the greater pressure outside the bottle drew the pus from the boil.

To cure hair infestation a small quantity of Quassia chips (bitter chips) were purchased from the chemist and boiled in vinegar. When the mixture had cooled a small-toothed comb was dipped into the mixture and drawn through the hair. The chips were also boiled in water and the solution used as a spray against greenfly!

To confirm that nursery rhymes often have a basis in fact, vinegar and brown paper were placed on the temples to counteract headaches.

For chest complaints camphorated oil, plus castor or olive oil was rubbed in. Goose grease was another remedy. Constipation had a number of reputed cures, the most popular being castor oil, liquorice powder, Flowers of Sulphur, chocolate laxative or Epsom Salts. Singly, of course.

A mixture of cold mustard applied to unbroken chilblains was said to get rid of the irritation while, for a sore throat, a tar-rope or old sock tied around the neck did the trick.

The cure for whooping cough involved a trip to Weston where the air from the incoming tide was reputed to be beneficial for the complaint.

For asthma sufferers to gain relief, first sheets of old blotting paper were cut into pieces about five inches square. 3d worth of Saltpetre was mixed with a pint of boiling water into which, when cool, the paper was dipped and then allowed to dry. At night several pieces of paper were ignited in the bedroom and the resulting fumes were said to ease the asthmatic's breathing. Unfortunately it did quite the reverse to any other occupants of the room.

Snails were crushed and rubbed on the chest to combat T.B., while leeches were applied to ease bruises and swellings. Parsley water kept the kidneys in good order and brimstone and treacle (commonly known as the 'Springtime mixture') was given to purify the blood.

5 Those who cared

In a way those who had the least money lived the most dearly. The local shop which allowed people to 'put it on the slate' until the end of the week encouraged a false economy. The single box of matches, the candle, the pint of paraffin, the small quantities of butter, bread and bacon cost dear when compared with the prices charged for the very same items bought by the dozen, the gallon or the pound. Storage problems for coal meant that only a hundredweight was bought at a time, brought from the local coal-yard in a borrowed handcart.

Cheap meat was available if you were prepared to walk the street of a Saturday night until the butchers decided to sell off their supplies at cut price rather than let them deteriorate over the weekend, for they had no facilities for cold storage. Generally, much use was made of tripe, cow's udder, melt, muggets, chitterling, sweetbreads, pig's trotters and pork bones stewed up with lentils. Stewed rabbit was high on the menu because of its comparative cheapness, as also were pig's tails. The odorous salted fish – toe-rag, named after a tramp's foot wrappings – was a favourite dish.

And, when times were really bad, there was always the pawnbroker.

'It was nothing for some to take clothes down to the pawnbroker's at the beginning of the week and get them out again for Sunday. For those who were ashamed to be seen going into the pawnbroker's there was a woman who used to take the stuff down for them. She charged them a few coppers. Those who took stuff themselves usually took it to a shop in another part of town where the neighbours wouldn't see them.'

During the winter months the Blanket Lending Society and other such organisations loaned out blankets to poor families. It was a standing joke amongst the more fortunate that some blankets need not be taken back – they could walk back unaided.

Poor children relied for 'new' boots upon charity organisations, or the Parish. The footwear was distinctive, usually having metal studded soles for longer wear.

'I used to envy some of the kids their charity boots and wished I had a pair because, when the kids slid along the road, the studs sent out a shower of sparks.'

A group of children in Waters' Place, c. 1930. The little boy in the front row, third from left, shows the metal-studded soles of his charity boots.

The older parts of Bedminster were well served by various churches and missions and these were the focal point for a way of life distinct from that of the local pub. For married women they offered a brief respite from overcrowded living conditions. For while, generally speaking, menfolk left the house each day, returning there for rest, as to a lesser degree did the children from school, the mothers' only recreation lay in the activities provided by religious organisations. Thus came the development of the Woman's Bright Hour, sewing circles and discussion groups.

The social activities centred around the Society of Friends' Princess Street Mission were varied and catered for the whole family.

Monday	Sewing class – Men's Mutual Improvement (Talks on various topics)
Tuesday	Temperance Meeting
Wednesday	Band of Hope – Prayer meeting
Thursday	Christian Endeavour
Friday	Open for AGM or special activity
Saturday	Coffee/Supper. Entertainment by members. Cup of tea and bun for one penny.
Sunday	Sunday School – Evening Service.

Other activities included games for children and a Girls' Choir was formed by Mrs Watson. She also introduced the idea of Woodcraft Folk to the district, an organisation featuring camping and folk dancing amongst other interests.

There was the inevitable football team.

St John's Mission Room, in Whitehouse Lane, was run by the Sisters of Mercy who were attached to the Bedminster Parish Church of St John's. Their headquarters was the House of Charity in West Street, opposite Sheene Road, from where they operated a soup distribution centre after the First World War. At the Mission Room they attended to the people's needs in general. The room was also used for old people's concerts and, in the 1930s, a Girl Guide group met there. In addition to this, the Sisters ran a nursery in nearby Percy Street and later became involved with St Agnes' Children's Home at Knowle. Emily Wring, formerly a cigar maker at Wills' Tobacco Factory, became housekeeper to the Kelham Fathers at St John's Church and later Superintendent of the St John's Mission, where she was assisted by Miss Marshall.

Before the outbreak of war in 1939 there was held each year, in June, the Patronal Festival. This consisted of a parade through Bedminster's streets similar to the beating of the bounds. The procession, made up almost entirely of children carrying flowers on sticks, was usually preceded by the local Salvation Army Band.

Bedminster Salvation Army Band in Leicester Street.

1981 sees the Salvation Army celebrating the Centenary of its work in Bedminster. While at first their work tended to be more evangelical than practical, in 1917 they set up their first Slum Post in a room over a chandler's shop in St Luke's Road, opposite the Council school.

The idea of the Slum Post was that the full-time Salvation Army officers should live in the same surroundings as the people they wished to help and to show, by personal example, that cleanliness and a moral way of life was possible under the circumstances. They did not, however, adopt a holier-than-thou attitude towards others, for it was realised that mothers, for example, who had been coping with a large family, squalid living conditions and other domestic problems were rather more inclined to drop to their knees with exhaustion rather than for prayer.

Generally they were successful in improving the life of the community where they worked and their range of involvement included: taking food to the aged and infirm; running soup kitchens; the distribution of blankets and extra clothing; grandfathers', women's and youth clubs; clinics; laying out the dead; holiday homes; deaf and dumb ministry; home crafts etc.

The St Luke's Road Post closed in 1920 and was transferred to Stillhouse Lane, behind a Bedminster Parade pawnshop. This, in turn, closed down about 1930 and a new Post was opened in Willway Street. The premises were an empty public house, the former *Willway Tavern*, and the skittle alley was used for prayer meetings. The Post remained here until the mid-1940s.

Bessie, now in her eighties, recalls an incident from her work at the Willway Street location:

'A man and his wife who worshipped at the Post had three children and the youngest, Amy, was a cripple. She was very deformed; her fingers were all curled up and she couldn't use them. She could only walk on her toes if someone held her. But, in spite of it all, she was a happy girl. On Sunday she went to the Penitent Form as she wanted to be saved; she couldn't kneel so she sat on the form. It was very touching to see her. Sometime later she died and as she had expressed the wish for an Army funeral, this was granted. (This took place sometime between 1925 and 1928.) Commandant Green and Ensign Rollason were the officers at the time.

'This funeral caused quite a sensation in Stillhouse Lane because I don't think the people watching had seen young lady bearers before. There were four of them. We walked by the side of the hearse, from Stillhouse Lane to the cemetery, then carried the coffin to the graveside. While we were sad at losing Amy, we were pleased to carry out this little duty.'

When areas ceased to be classified as 'slummy', the ordinary Field Corps of the Army took over. Later, Goodwill Centres superseded the old Slum Posts.

Most people's memories of the Salvation Army will be of its band. During the 1930s the Bedminster Army Band played every Saturday night in the vicinity of East Street, drawing onlookers from the late-night shoppers. Often the crowds caused traffic congestion and shop-keepers complained to the police. But when the latter ordered the band to move elsewhere the public demanded they be allowed to remain and the Army band continued to play in Church Road until the outbreak of war in 1939.

It is the Army's boast that there are few streets and roads in Bedminster where the band has neither played, nor marched through. A band was formed, not long after the formation of the Bedminster Corps itself, by Billy Mann and two other members. Soon, other enthusiasts had joined the three until there were 25 potential bandsmen. They were provided with instruments and within three weeks of the band's inauguration were playing in public.

Band historian, the late Tom Cable, and a former bandsman himself records:

'Not having played an instrument before, these men produced an awful, but spirited noise, unto the Lord.'

Up to the present day the band has played under twelve bandmasters, perhaps the best known being George Fox.

6 This sporting life

At the turn of the century and after, Bedminster produced its share of boxers. One of the best amateurs at bantam-weight was Alf Advent. At feather- and light-weight was Harry Mansfield, good enough to have a decision over champion Jim Driscoll. One of the many booths at which Mansfield fought was Bill Moore's, in the Horsefair. Tragically, Mansfield died of T.B. in Philip Street, Bedminster, not far from Willway Street, where there lived a boxing contemporary of his, 'Deppy' Thomas. Deppy's son, Bert, was also to become a well-known local boxer after the First World War.

During the twenties and thirties boxing was held at a variety of venues in Bedminster and many of the aspiring boxers frequenting the halls and booths came into the area from Wales. Unemployed and practically destitute, they chose to employ their natural fighting abilities to make money. But it was a venture not without danger for men who lacked stamina through ill-nourishment and lack of training. Usually the most they could do was put up a good show against the booth professional and ensure a good 'nobbing' for their efforts at the end of the bout. But a hard-pressed professional, obliged to fight back to save both job and reputation, was always capable of administering temporary or even permanent injury to such challengers. For these were hungry times and even the professional had to live.

The main promoters of boxing in Bedminster were the Norton brothers, Eddie and Bill Rowlands, Bill Bosch, Albert Rawlings and Jack Rose. The boxing referee, Albert Jennings, was associated with these in the promotion of fights at the Original Bedminster Boxing Club.

Important bouts took place in the Bedminster Arcade. This glass-roofed walk-way between the old Stoll Picture Theatre and Woolworths, extended from East Street through to Catherine Mead Street. From the East Street entry the Boxing Hall was on the right-hand side, up two flights of stairs.

Len Munden, now a coach proprietor and one of Bristol's few remaining pre-war boxers, fought his first professional bout at Bedminster in 1930, against Billy Davis. The purse was ten shillings.

Lesser bouts took place at a small leather warehouse to the rear of the old Rex Cinema; Milton's Hall in Essex Street; the Ford Memorial Hall, Mill Lane and at show booths such as that at the Red Cow Yard in West Street, where Sammy McGiven was the proprietor. Open-air boxing was sometimes held on the Bristol City Football Ground.

Bedminster has seen the development of its very own football team and Bristol City's failures and good fortunes have been assiduously followed since just before the turn of the century.

Originally Bristol South End, the club was formed in 1894 and the first General Meeting was held at *The General Elliot* public house in East Street, Bedminster. At first the team played on a ground behind *The Engineer's Arms*, St John's Lane (now *The House That Jack Built*).

In 1897 Bristol South End became Bristol City and was elected to the Southern League. Three years later it amalgamated with its local rival team, Bedminster, and while games were still played on the St John's Lane

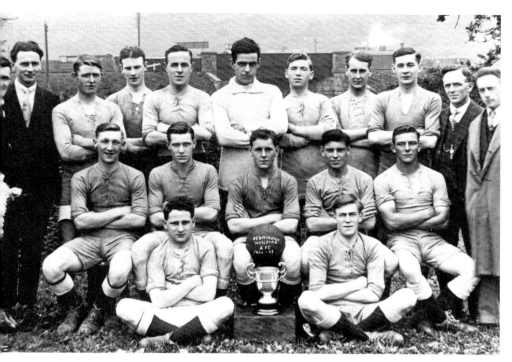

The Bedminster Wesleyan A.F.C. 1926-27: (back row, left to right) K. Frieze, H. Chappell, G. Bolt, W. Winfield, R. Selway, S. Neale, L. Rowlands, T. Wedlock, P. Blakes, F. Smith, H. Mathews; (middle row) W. Smith, F. Weston, J. Wedlock, F. Wedlock, D. Cook; (front) E. Southway, A. Horler.

ground, the preferred Ashton Gate location, with its stand, eventually became the team's permanent headquarters.

The greatest occasion for the followers of Bristol football came in 1935, when City had a fantastic run in the Cup. They first beat Gillingham, Rotherham and Bury (after two replays), then came up against First Division Portsmouth. A goal-less draw at Fratton Park brought a mid-week replay to Ashton Gate.

In anticipation of the 'Cup Fever' generated locally by the coming replay, all Wednesday League games in the area were cancelled and several large firms gave their workers time off to attend the match. Wills' employees had been on short time, not having worked the previous two Saturdays, so the firm closed down Wednesday afternoon and the lost time was made up the following Saturday. John Cox, the tanners, let their employees start work earlier at six a.m., finishing at 2 p.m. City offices closed, employees returning to work after the match to make up time.

The gates at the City Ground were opened at 1 o'clock and remained open until kick off at 2.30 p.m. As mid-day approached, the roads leading to Ashton began to fill with groups of young City supporters, proudly displaying their team's colours, wearing comic hats and home-made costumes; waving on high their 'Up the Robins' banners.

The noisy, high-spirited throng converged upon the entrance gate of the ground. They had walked, come by coach, car or bicycle. Many of the cyclists, as was customary, parked their machines in the front gardens of houses near the ground and were charged a few coppers for the privilege. Portsmouth fans made the journey north by coach or in the two special excursion trains.

For long periods the traffic stopped and it was difficult to progress towards the ground. Hundreds of cars were parked in all the available spaces in the Ashton Gate area. The scene reminded older fans of the City's pre-war First Division grandeur.

Ten minutes before kick-off long queues were still striving to gain entrance; many fans had taken refuge upon the roofs of the grandstands. There was a mighty cheer when the City team of Dolman, Roberts and Bridge; Riley, Pearce and Binton; Hodge, Banfield, Harston, Landell and Cainey took the field. They were accompanied by the *Evening Post* mascot, Murphy, looking, if anything, slightly grotesque in wide-striped trousers, frock coat, decorated bowler and Charlie Chaplin moustache.

So great was the crush that soon after the match started barricades gave way and several thousand spectators were precipitated onto the pitch. Some were slightly injured in the process. The referee had to hold up play until the crowd were retrenched four or five deep behind the touchline.

Police reinforcements summoned to prevent spectators encroaching on the field of play were kept well occupied. When a corner was forced an avenue had to be made in the crowd before a player could take the kick.

Meanwhile, despite the efforts of officials and police, many thousands crashed through one of the entrance gates and gained free admittance.

When Bristol City scored their first goal, wildly cheering supporters surged onto the pitch. Jubilant enthusiasts could be heard for miles.

City won 2-0 and the recorded attandance was 42,885. They then qualified to play Preston North End in the next round.

Well anticipating the City win, Mr Reg Bennett, Managing Director of Knowle Greycing Stadium, and a keen soccer fan, while compiling his card for the Wednesday meeting decided to call the last race the 'Preston North End Handicap'.

Unfortunately for City, Preston North End proved to be just that for their Cup aspirations. There was a hard fought goal-less draw at Ashton Gate but Bristol City were well beaten 5-0 on Preston's home turf in the replay.

For many a day, the Portsmouth match was 'replayed' again and again in Billy Wedlock's *Star Inn* – just across the road from where Billy himself gave so many memorable performances as a member of the City team. Several ex-City players kept public houses in Bedminster. Paddy O'Brien *The Packet* in Coronation Road; Joe Cottle *The Exchange Hotel* in East Street and later *The Leicester House* in Leicester Street.

Before the days of the *Pink 'Un* and *Green 'Un*, some Bedminster newsagents displayed the late football results in their shop windows on Saturday evenings.

Greyhound racing came to Knowle on Saturday, July 27th, 1927, when a crowd of between seven and eight thousand attended the first greyhound meeting there. Nearly 100 bookmakers were on the course.

It was reputed to be the best laid out track in England. The Directors of Wembley Stadium showed interest in the electric hare system which had been installed and later placed an order with Charles Hill and Sons for a similar system to be put in at London. Obviously proud of the Stadium's early recognition, in 1930 the directors installed a new type of trap which gave a better and fairer start to all dogs.

In late 1928 the Bristol Dirt Track was opened at the Knowle Stadium. The Bristol Inter-City team who rode against Manchester at this meeting were L. Parker, F. Smith and S. Gill.

Len Parker was the most successful rider at the meeting and, for winning the Golden Helmet Race, he was presented with the Golden Helmet Award by Mr Harry Tate, the comedian. A photograph in the Bristol Observer shows him seated on his machine, being congratulated by Mr W. Douglas, whose bikes were used by the riders.

Bristol Bulldogs, as the team later became known, entered the Provincial League in the late thirties and, in their heyday, attracted larger crowds than Bristol City.

Greyhound Racing also took place on the Magnet Track at South Liberty Lane, Bedminster. It was known as a 'Flapping Track', the name generally given to unlicensed tracks where stringent regulations did not apply and where abuses and irregularities were common. The Magnet's name is supposed to have come from the magnet shape of the track itself.

The Bedminster Track was first opened in June, 1928 and there were about 2,000 persons present – people who paid to go in, that is, for the track could be viewed at a distance from the top of an old South Liberty Pit slag-heap, or the side of Bedminster Down. Those watching in this fashion often had a penny or two on the races between themselves. A close finish inevitably led to arguments as to which dog had won.

At first the track was run by a Mr Northcott and then by one of showman Charlie Heal's sons. It was the latter who replaced the old hand-powered, bicycle wheel lure winder with a steam engine.

It has been suggested that punters frequenting Billy Wedlock's pub at Ashton Gate were often able to pick up tips as to possible winners. Some of the dog-owners came through this way en route to the Magnet Track. As they passed by their cronies they would give an almost imperceptible thumbs up or down sign, to let them know whether or not it was their dog's turn to win or lose. Sometimes a dog would be conditioned to lose the race by being given a good drink of water, or the owner would buy a couple of pork pies and sit outside the pub feeding his dog with them. But, on one occasion, this method did not work on the favourite – who overcame its pork-pie handicap and went on to win, leaving the owner and others 'in the know' as sorry losers.

In the latter years of the Magnet (it closed in 1932) the evening's sport began with a whippet race. This was rather appropriate as rabbit coursing, using whippets, was a favourite sport amongst the mining fraternity employed at South Liberty Pit. They also indulged in the repulsive spectacle of cock-fighting.

Percy Still of the Bristol South Cycling Club came first in this race at Ashton Gate in 1925. Marley Brice of Bath Cycling Club was second and Claud Boulton third.

Bedminster Cricket Club was formed in 1847 and has had a long and interesting history. When Bedminster played West Gloucestershire in September 1855, on Durdham Down, four of the Grace family played for the opposing team.

E. M. Grace played for Bedminster in 1857 and in 1865 the Grand Old Man himself, W. G. Grace, played for Bedminster against Ashton, scoring 28 out of a total of 131. In later years the Graces played for Bedminster on many occasions. W.G.'s only recorded pair of ducks was made in the Bedminster v. Swindon match at Greenway Bush Lane.

At the beginning of the century the club lost their ground and for some seasons played on the Bristol City Football Ground. In 1912 the lease of the Clanage, from the Smyth Estate, gave the club the ground which they were to call their own.

7 Entertainment

A great deal of free entertainment came from local sport. The majority of clubs were linked to the various factories, or associated with churches, chapels and missions. During the football season it was a familiar sight to see various teams, clad in their team colours, clunking through the streets in their leather-studded boots, sometimes having to walk a considerable distance from changing room to pitch. In addition to the adult leagues there was a variety of schoolboy teams competing for the Woodcock Shield.

One local football team – that of the East Street Football Club – also became known for entertainment off the field when, in 1927, members of the club formed the nucleus of the East Street Baptist Male Voice Choir. Mr W. G. Mills was its first conductor and the choir won several trophies at local Eisteddfods. One of the better-known local choirs, it is still going strong today.

Showyards attracted many people. The young with little money were drawn there by the noise of the steam organ and the polished glitter of the Noah's Ark and roundabouts. They saw their more affluent elders pushing pennies into the money-greedy mouths of inviting slot machines which, on occasion, reluctantly disgorged the gambler's money, or conceded a free go. The hoop-la stalls with prizes which always seemed larger than the rings meant to encircle them. The rifle range with its targets of ping-pong balls rising and falling on currents of air. The coconut shies where the nuts snuggled down in sawdust-filled cups and disdainfully resisted the wooden balls blasted at them.

One showman of the period was Mr Marshall who used a yard to the rear of Wills' factory. The Marshall family lived in New Charlotte Street, not far from the yard and close to Bedminster Police Station. It was on their showground that Billy Butlin began his career with a merry-go-round. Part of his early education was received at Redcliffe School.

Another family concern was Charles Heal who, together with Rogers and Saunders (his sons-in-law), usually had a show at the Red Cow Yard, just off West Street.

Other locations for these shows were near Locks Mills, Ashton Park and Robinson's Sports Ground in St. John's Lane.

A favourite haunt of younger men and youths, especially during the dark, winter months, was Parker's Billiard Hall, just off East Street. The charge was one shilling and sixpence an hour. The tables were on two floors; those upstairs generally reserved for novices and showing their age by the worn, near springless cushions and patched cloth. On the ground floor were the better tables and No 1 table was the best of the lot. Here the semi-professionals played, watched by the older men. Old men who watched knowingly, puffing gently on their shag-filled pipes which they removed, at intervals, to eject spittle into the spittoons placed at intervals on the floor. The atmosphere was cosy, with the sharp click of the balls and tobacco smoke rising from the table-lit areas towards the darkened ceiling. A world apart from normal life outside.

For those disinclined to a 'mis-spent youth', there were many dance-halls in the district. Some of the church-halls held dances while the best-known halls were the Imperial, Milton's and the Ford Memorial Hall in Mill Lane. There was also one behind the Town Hall Cinema. They were well patronised and entrance fees varied from sixpence to a shilling. Fairly long frocks were worn by the girls until the coming of the 'Black Bottom' and the 'Charleston' created a fashion for short dresses and long strings of beads.

Still going strong in 1937, Bristol South Cycling Club stop for elevenses at Bridgwater. Ten members have been identified: B. Preston, E. Janes, A. Cook, E. Ilot, T. Carberry, J. Pegler, N. Broomfield, R. Deane, P. Jefferies and B. Sullivan.

In the summer months camping, hiking and cycling were popular pursuits and these clubs often had social overtones.

Bristol South Cycling Club began in April 1893 when a group of cycling enthusiasts met at Heaven's Coffee Tavern, Hill Avenue, Victoria Park. It was first suggested, because of the large number of W.D. & H.O. Wills employees among the members, that the Club be named the 'W.D. & H.O. Wills's Cycling Club'. But realising how this would restrict future membership, 'Bristol South Cycling Club' was finally decided upon.

By the turn of the century there were about 30 cycling clubs in Bristol but the Bristol South C.C. was the only local club to survive the 1914-18 war.

Distinguished members of the twenties and thirties were Ernie Warbutton, unbeaten in local championship racing between 1919 and 1926, while George Hill was his worthy successor. During the period between the wars the club was very active, winning the Frampton Memorial Shield outright, and re-presenting it to the N.C.U. for further competitions. It was also the founder club of the Western Time Trials Association, while its evening track sports were a popular feature in Bristol fixtures. The members were strong supporters of the Youth Hostel Association as an aid to touring.

The club is still active and its members, both men and women, proudly carry forward the traditions of yesterday.

The closure of the old Picturedrome in Bedminster Parade left Bedminster with two picture houses after the war: the Town Hall, in Cannon Street, and the Bedminster Hippodrome in East Street. As the admission charge to the Town Hall was less than that of the Hippodrome, at first the Town Hall was the more popular of the two. Most people familiar with the years between the wars will remember the cinema through the eyes of a child. They will also have experienced the growth of the film from its silent days, with piano accompaniment, to the glittering presentation of the American musical, with its full orchestration and dancing and singing stars.

In the early days both cinemas had occasional live shows during the intervals and the Hippodrome had amateur talent shows on Sunday evenings. But for many the most vivid memories will be of the 'Two-penny Rush'. This showing was originally held on Saturday afternoons at the Town Hall, then later became a permanent Saturday morning excursion. The clients for this show were almost entirely children, intent upon seeing the adventures of their cowboy heroes – Tom Mix, Ken Maynard, Buck Jones and later Bill Boyd (Hopalong Cassidy) and Gene Autry. These he-men seldom, if ever, kissed the heroine.

A favourite buy for children to take to the pictures was a penny-worth of 'pinky' fruit. This was the name given to apples, oranges, bananas and grapes which were either over-ripe or badly bruised so as to make them unsaleable in the normal way. At the cinema all the good parts of the fruit were eaten and the repulsive debris saved until the lights began to dim. It was then thrown in a wild fusilade across the cinema, either at random or at a pre-selected target.

'I remember on one occasion the film had started while I was still picking over a bunch of grapes. The lad in front of me impeded my view with his excited jumping up and down. Incensed at his being responsible for my having missed a particularly exciting incident, I pushed the remaining grapes onto his seat. He came down with a squelch, thought the worst had happened, and remained transfixed for several minutes before plucking up enough courage to discover what had occurred. I felt justice had been done'.

Crowds wait outside the Town Hall in Cannon Street to see a silent film. There were frequent fights to get in before a queue system was enforced. (1920s).

Fruit coster in East Street, 1935 — a possible source of the 'pinky' fruit often bought by children going to the cinema.

It was not uncommon for the projector to break down. Boos and jeers would come from the audience and the manager would get onto the stage in front of the screen and threaten to throw everyone out unless they behaved. Sometimes he would try, unsuccessfully, to start a sing-song. The worst position in the cinema was in the rear seats for here the view of the screen was restricted by the tall pillars supporting the balcony. In addition, the ever-burning gas jets were at their brightest so that misbehaviour could easily be identified by the attendants.

Quite a few children deserted the Town Hall when the Hippodrome started its own 'Saturday Morning Picture Club'. Not only did it offer prizes to its club members but also, when it first opened, gave away small gifts such as trick rubber-lead pencils and large balloons.

The children's interest in cowboys was taken advantage of by some mothers who made 'cowboy' trousers from old flour sacks by part slitting them down the middle, then sewing them up as legs. It was an opportunity to protect the child's school clothes from undue wear and tear.

The Bedminster Hippodrome in East Street, which was blitzed in 1940.

A street party in 1918 — Phipps Street, Ashton.

The most popular street games were Hopscotch, Queeny Ball, O'Reilly Says, Statues, Skipping, Hoops, Marbles, Generals, Puss-in-the-Corner, Tally-Ho, Knock-out-Ginger, Tip-Stick, Kick-tin and Tops.

Children were given tea and Christmas parties by churches, chapels and missions and also trips to the seaside. Their elders went on charabanc outings with church, club or pub. Or, as in January 1935, they would be given free entertainment. In this instance by Mr W. E. Gardner, of Granby House, who celebrated his 84th birthday by inviting 200 old people, all over 70, to a 'tea and social' at the Ford Memorial Hall.

Club outing: to Weymouth with the East Street Cycling Club (1925).

Church outing: to Cheddar with the East Street Baptist Young Men's Bible Class (1927).

Pub outing: with ladies from the New Pilgrim, Stillhouse Lane in the 1920s (publican Lilian Frost).

8 South Bristol Central School

On September 1st, 1919, began an experiment in a new type of education with the opening of the Bristol Central Schools. There were three of these schools, East, North and South; the two former being co-educational.

Created to fill a gap between Secondary and Elementary schools, they catered for those children who had just failed to qualify for Secondary education, but were considered suitable for a higher education than that provided by the Elementary school. The curriculum was geared towards technical and commercial skills.

South Bristol Central School took over the old buildings of what had formerly been Bedminster Down Elementary School. The original red-brick building being insufficient for the needs of the new school, several ex-army huts were erected in the playground.

The subjects taught were composition and grammar; arithmetic and algebra; geometry, French; science; art; literature; history; geography and scripture; engineering drawing, metalwork and woodwork. During the school term visits were made to local industries. There was an annual outing to Clevedon and, in later years, excursions abroad.

South Bristol Central football team, 1925-26.

At first, school inspectors were inclined to be critical of both masters and boys as they struggled with a new environment. However, by the mid-1920s, the school had laid the foundation for the traditions that were to be uniquely its own.

In sport, especially football, they were most fortunate in having George Crandon as one of the teachers. A key figure in local football (he was the South-West representative on the English Schools' F.A. Council), under his expert eye the school was successful in winning the Woodcock Shield. During his eleven years at the school George Crandon began his association with Bristol City, later becoming a director, and in his first team he had an ex-South Bristol Central boy, Jimmy Heale.

The school ran its own orchestra and this later provided the musical accompaniment to the school's productions of Gilbert and Sullivan opera. Performances began in 1925 with *Trial by Jury* and the novelty of schoolboys playing female roles was soon overcome by the quality of the production. The scenery, properties and wigs were made by the boys under the supervision of the masters. Mr Fussell and Mr Surtees produced and directed the operas up to Mr Fussell's leaving in 1930, when his place was adequately filled by Mr Scillitoe. The operas were produced every year, the last *The Gondoliers* in 1939.

The school buildings had been unsuitable from the start, being cramped and badly-drained. In 1936 the school was transferred to Castle Green School and, yet again, to Bedminster Bridge School, Stillhouse Lane in 1939. The Central Schools were disbanded, together with Temple Technical School, during this year and the pupils were given the choice of going to either the newly formed Junior Technical School (Stillhouse Lane and Temple Back) or the Junior Commercial School, at Castle Green.

South Bristol Central School had begun at the end of one war and closed at the beginning of another. The majority who attended the school and helped create its tradition, remember it with affection and pride.

9 Characters and Eccentrics

The characters of a community add colour to the streets and, in so doing, help create that community's own identity.

There was Mrs White, who sold wet fish from her barrow in a narrow recess, leading to a tannery, just off East Street, wearing a man's cap and boots. Or 'Granny' Wookey, the small-time haulier, who sat perched on her cart with an old Victorian bonnet on her head and white stockings on her legs. Lil Saunders chopped wood, then pushed it around the streets in a cart to sell it.

Of the many newspaper sellers the most widely known character was Freddie Kent. With chunky figure draped in a long, black coat and the ever-present bowler hat, with raucous voice he shouted his wares.

'Cloggy' Davis owned a boot shop in East Street until he sold up and took a small lock-up shed-cum-shop in Church Lane. He specialised in making the heavy clogs such as worn by the tannery workers. Bobby Bennett pushed a handcart about the district, buying up old woollens and jam-jars, or you could take them to his premises in Whitehouse Street.

'Dixie' Brown, the coloured, blind ex-boxer, could be seen being led about by one or another of his children, his short days of courage and glory gone, though remembered by some.

Polly Reynolds – whose bearded husband played the trombone in the local Salvation Army Band – served in her second-hand clothes shop in West Street. She handed out religious texts like Green Shield stamps. In the shop window was an opened bible and she turned the pages to a new lesson each day. When she died her daughter took her place.

Not far away, in Rowley Street, lived 'Professor' Gibbs. When he went out he kept his normally long, flowing hair tucked up under an old Homburg hat and wore his ankle-length raincoat throughout the year, no matter the weather. His feet were enclosed in an over-sized pair of boots with toes that turned up. His footwear, more often than not, was given to him by Polly Reynolds. In his younger days he had a reputation as a great walker. The outstanding feat for which he is remembered is his walk from Bedminster Bridge to Weston and back – twice in the same day! Local people swore by the accuracy of his weather forecasts.

If you wanted a horoscope, 'Captain' Butler was your man at his pitch in Warden road.

It is not too great a step from these minor characters to the true eccentric and Bedminster has been graced with its share of eccentrics, at least from the 18th century onwards.

In the early part of the 18th century the Rev. Emanuel Collins brought notoriety to Bedminster by keeping an inn *The Sign of the Duke of Marlborough*, performing illegal marriages and for his satirical verse and other writings.

The 19th century gave Bedminster 'Caraboo'. This was the name given to Mary Baker (born Mary Wilcocks) who, after a colourful career, turned up at Almondsbury, Gloucestershire, in 1817, disguised as an Eastern princess. Her deceit was discovered but she was forgiven and a benefactor paid her passage to America.

Mary Baker returned to England in 1834 and sometime between that date and 1851, came to live in Bedminster with her daughter. She was a dealer in leeches until her death in 1864.

Still remembered by many of Bedminster's older residents is Charlie Stephens, the Bedminster barber who attempted to 'shoot' the Niagara Falls in a wooden barrel.

The Stephens family originated from South Wales and, prior to coming to Bristol, they had seven lodgers. One of these was Jack James, father of John James the Bristol millionaire, who at one time lived in Philip Street, Bedminster.

Charlie Stephens was 58 years of age at the time of his attempt, had seen 3½ years war service and boasted, in addition to his war medals, five gold and six silver medals for various daring achievements. These included kissing lions in their den; shaving customers in a lion's cage, boxing in a lion's cage; standing before American knife-throwers and also having an apple cut in two on his throat, by a sword; snatching a would-be suicide from death on a railway line by so narrow a margin that the train, in passing, cut the woman's skirt from her body; making parachute descents from a balloon.

For his parachute descents he wore a red coat. Both parachutes and balloons were made by a man named Spencer. Once he jumped from a balloon, over Bristol City Football Ground, and landed in Chessel Street where he was picked up by local dairyman Harry Wookey. On another occasion he landed on Bedminster Railway Station. His wife, Anne, not to be outdone, went up to 5,000 feet in a balloon, receiving a certificate for doing so.

The barrel in which the attempt was to be made was constructed by a Bath cooper. With special fittings and other refinements it cost over £20. There was little room for manoeuvre inside. Charlie Stephens was 5ft 9 inches in height and the barrel was 6ft 2 inches in length, 32 inches in the middle, tapering off to about 26 inches at either end. It was reinforced by ten stout, metal hoops and had a lid which could be released from inside by means of a screw-wheel. A small electric light was installed which gave a glimmer for up to eight hours.

The total weight of the barrel, with its 2 inch thick oak staves was around 6 cwt. Of this one cwt was a solid iron plate and, in addition, there was a 60 lb lump of lead for balance. Thus weighted it was thought the barrel would remain vertical in the water.

Stephen's arms and feet were secured by straps, while a waist-band was expected to minimise concussion. Breathing apparatus, similar to the First World War gas-mask, was also available.

Prior to leaving for Niagara Falls on June 18th, 1920, Charlie Stephens exhibited his barrel in Old Market, Bristol, charging the townspeople a small fee to help cover his expenses. When he had first considered the expedition some 11 years earlier, Stephens was unsuccessful in persuading a film company to cover the stunt. However, before leaving England, he was delighted to hear that the editor of a Toronto newspaper had negotiated with a Canadian film company on his behalf. This would more than reimburse him the £140 it had already cost.

Stephens had been advised by many of his friends not to make the

The Stephens family. The ill-fated Charlie is seated mid-front. The others are: (back row from left) Florrie, Lily, Ada, Annie, Alice and Charlie Junior; (front row) Rose, Viola, Charlie, Viola (grandchild), Anne (Charlie's wife) and Bert. The picture was taken just before Charlie left for the Niagara Falls.

attempt and, in Canada, Bobby Leach – an English stuntman who had successfully jumped the Falls in 1911, in a steel drum – tried to persuade Stephens against the venture. Leach's main objection was against the amount of weight being carried at the bottom of the barrel for, it is recorded, in addition to the original weights, Charles Stephens intended tying an anvil to his feet. But Stephens would not be persuaded, perhaps thinking Leach was jealous he might succeed.

At ten minutes past eight on Sunday morning, July 11th, the barrel containing Charles Stephens was released in the river two miles above the Falls. Its progress was watched by a few friends and recorded by a photographer, as they followed the bobbing barrel in motor cars along the river's edge.

The barrel neared the brink of the watery slope, hesitated for a moment, then slid over the edge of the abyss. Its black and red sides could still be seen half-way down the cataract, then it was lost to view in the swirling spray. Unknown to the spectators, the over-weighted barrel had dropped through the water and crashed upon the jagged rocks at the foot of the Falls. Men stationed below waited in vain for the barrel to appear. Crowds gazed expectantly from the banks and the arch of the bridge but, after an hour or so, it was decided that Charles Stephens had failed in his ambition.

Later, all that was found was a tattoed arm strapped to a piece of the barrel and several wooden remnants.

To add to the tragedy a telegram which should have been sent to Anne, his wife, giving news of the success or failure of the mission, was never sent. Stephens' wife first heard of his death from newspaper reports. Later came the distressing advice from Canada that a £20 payment for the photographic record of Charles Stephens' last great adventure, had been just sufficient to cover the cost of burying his arm!

After her husband's death Anne Stephens employed a man to carry on her husband's barbering business. Later she bought her son, Bertie, out of the Navy and he took over. Her younger son, Charlie, opened a ladies' hair-dressers.

It is not likely that anyone this century will better the deeds of Charlie Stephens, but one wonders who, now alive or to be born in the future, will take on the mantle of the Bedminster eccentric in the 21st century?

Other titles published by Redcliffe Press
on behalf of Bristol & West Building Society:

The Bristol Scene

Views of Bristol by Bristol artists from the collection of the City Art
Gallery, with text by Jennifer Gill. First published in 1973, this popular
'bestseller' has recently been re-issued. 6 pages in full colour, and many
black and white illustrations. *Price: £1.25*

Victorian Buildings in Bristol

Clare Crick's authoritative and highly praised study of Bristol's rich legacy
of Victorian architecture. Already a standard reference work on the
subject. Profusely illustrated. *Price: £1.75*

Changing Bristol: new architecture and conservation 1960-1980

Architectural writer Tony Aldous examines the best of the city's modern
buildings and conservation schemes of the past 20 years. The study is fully
illustrated with 40 black and white photographs. *Price: £1.95*

Publication Summer 1982:

Brunel in Bristol by Angus Buchanan

An illustrated study of the impact on Bristol of the celebrated Victorian
engineer, with special reference to Clifton Suspension Bridge, s.s. Great
Britain and Temple Meads Railway Station. *Price: around £3.00*